Jack and Jill in Troy

Jack and Jill in Troy

Bob Perelman

For Juliana

best,

Bob

ROOF BOOKS
NEW YORK

ISBN: 978-1-931824-82-8
Library of Congress Control Number: 2019947056
Cover art by Francie Shaw

Thanks to Rae Armantrout, Alan Bernheimer, Brandon Brown,
George Mattingly, Francie Shaw and Susan Stewart for suggestions.

This book is made possible, in part, by the New
York State Council on the Arts with the support of
Governor Andrew Cuomo and the New York State Legislature.

Roof Books
are published by
Segue Foundation
300 Bowery, New York, NY 10012
seguefoundation.com

Roof Books
are distributed by
Small Press Distribution
1341 Seventh Street
Berkeley, CA. 94710-1403
800-869-7553 or spdbooks.org

This book is dedicated to Francie Shaw.

CLASSIC SUNRISE

Red-nosed dawn arose
—but it had been worth it!

All those gulps and gasps
had made the edges

of her eyes so sharp
that now when she finally

did heave herself up out of
the tossing sea

barely into
the eggshell sky

temples throbbing
—that goes without saying

without saying without saying—
she could see

all that was not her,
see the immortal not-self

perfectly, as in a spotless mirror.

THE ARMOR-SWAP

The older poet red in neck and face:
you can't talk about Homer that way!

it's *history!*
like his head was going to explode.

When, in fact, writing
an insulting but abortive challenge

from Diomedes the Greek
to Glaucon the Trojan

as they come together in battle,
Diomedes trolling,

Excuse me,
but have we *met?*

I'm more or less notorious
in front of Troy, you might say

I've spent serious time
in the hotspots, but I don't think

I've ever seen *you* before . . .
Glaucon, though, doesn't bite,

he sidesteps, musing about trees,
so leafy one minute,

bare branches the next,
and we're each one leaf,

and since you say
we haven't met,

here's my entire ancestry,
which takes awhile

but it eventually turns out
that the ancestors

of empathetic biothinker Glaucon
and the ancestors

of sneering warrior Diomedes
were, way back, genuine allies

and this new aspect to the situation
so enthuses D

that he stabs his spear into the ground
and hugs long-lost cousin G,

telling him you go kill other
Greeks and I'll kill other Trojans

but between you and me
there's perfect peace,

and this in turn so enthuses G
that in a spasm of witless bonhomie,

he swaps armor with his new friend,
gold armor for bronze,

as moronic as trading
a Maserati for a Civic,

Zeus having shortcircuited his thinking.
It must have been fun writing that

or however it happened.

THE KEEP

Jack and Jill went up the hill
to the windy keep of Troy.

This was long before
apnea set in and all our woe.

The keep is where
you keep things,

things of value,
cataloged carefully,

no matter whose they used to be,
which eventually makes for

provenance problems
up and down the hill,

big ones, little itches
dogging you

into every enclave,
nagging like a summer cold

when you're not young,
when someone's got

what's yours, has it,
up on the windy keep,

up whatever, the thought roots ·
and won't be budged:

that certain someone
is getting decimated,

him and all his glittering connections.

FOLK WISDOM

The mind they say
is like a clit

or supernatural fingertip
a sensitivity

far beyond
the spurious permanence

of names
and the best thing or at least

the best thing so far
is that this unavoidable sensitivity

leaves everything
up in the air

for the newcomers
the not-yet-speaking

the infants.

APHRODITE AND HELEN

It's private
what we're talking about

but everybody sees it.
The dictionary meaning

of the next word is aroused
but don't you think

in context angry
makes better sense?

Instantly Helen knew
the goddess' neck,

her whole being
through the disguise

of the old woman,
faithful wool-carder,

the one she loved most
back in Sparta.

But this was someone
quite different

and Helen
cut through the disguise,

raising her voice to Aphrodite.
Listen, I tell you it enrages me.

Each time you get total access
to everything I ever felt.

You dandle that thin chain
hanging from nowhere

all the way down to nursing
then you get to shove me

back into the fucking bedroom
and there's the airhead lover

fondling his armor
always the same grin

each time he sees me.

MISTER BIG

Menelaus, the deathless gods kept you in mind.
Athena protected you from that arrow.

She stood in front of you and saved your life,
brushing the bloodthirsty thing away

like a mother flicks a fly
away from the baby

she's finally gotten to sleep.

She nudged that arrow toward your belt,
where it slammed through the buckle,

gold of course, then shoving
through the tough outer cloth,

on through the pricey linen,
at last grazing your thigh

where the blood immediately
gushed out.

Think of the best Phoenician cheek-piece,
hand-stained deep purple in Maeonia

and which you now have
in your keep,

curated professionally.
Any serious horseman

would want it,
but it's yours,

ready to give
you and your horse glory

whenever you ride.
Think of that deep purple

one-of-a-kind thing
and it'll give you

an inkling, Menelaus,
how your bright blood

stained your big thighs
and kept dripping down

onto your exceptional ankles.

PAGANISM FOR DUMMIES

First lesson: Lessons are for dummies.

A life of wake up you're late
for your lesson. Think about it:

how many lessons are there going to be?
If they're never going to end, what's the point?

As opposed to the gods
with their—not superpowers exactly,

more like an absolutely upper hand,
free to appear or not,

answer prayers or not,
wield special effects,

knock down any structure,
whisk favorites out of danger.

They're on top, superlative beings
never wrong for long.

The problem is their names.
And of course the toga situation.

But the names are bad enough.
These days Zeus only works

if you're naming a dachshund.
Though that's not totally fair:

in their enclave, the gods
do remain skilled workers,

troopers, believable in every scene,
now observing from high distances,

now throwing their weight around,
even getting bent out of shape

when it says to in the script.
I.e., Zeus weeping over Sarpedon,

a favorite human son dead,
and he weeps bloody tears,

real ones. No one else does that.
But that's not to say human death

on an epic scale
teaches the gods anything at all —

far from it.
In general they could care less.

It's us getting the hard ones:
if you want your son's body back

then you kiss the hand
that killed him and dragged

the corpse around obsessively.
You kiss the hand

because you need the body,
because a funeral

is not legitimate
without the body.

If you learn nothing else,
get that through your head.

ALL-PURPOSE DISASTER POEM

It's your fucking fault
that it's like this.

Hand me the remote, would you?
Do you need another? I'm having one.

It wasn't ever like this
and now it's always like this
and it's your fucking fault.

Before, nobody imagined anything like this
but now, nobody can think anything else
and it's your—let's just leave it,
but we can't just leave it
and that's your fucking fault.

Not that I'm blaming you.
There was nothing you could do, really.
The friend of my enemy's bff
who just happens to be the boss's lapdog
and one fine day some drone
just happens to blow him to shreds.
And there's really nothing anyone could have done
or have not done
so who's to know
and that it's that random
is your fucking fault.

Hand me the remote, would you?
When did the guy say he'd be here?
Two hours ago. Right?
And he's bringing . . . what? *Coors?*
Coors *Lite?* Honestly,

fuck you. *I* would never, you're saying *I*
ordered Coors Lite? You can't be serious.
Give me the remote. Mad Men's on.

Remember when they tried to cancel
the Sixties? They're always trying to
cancel the Sixties. The Sixties are dead.
Deader than psychedelic rock. And whose fault is that?
Whose fault is it that nature
pisses off my white-identified neighbor?
Think, because it didn't just happen
that it'll never snow enough
to cool down my being pissed off
and that's your fucking fault.

Of course I walked around
in my red corduroy bellbottoms.
Wherever I wanted to go.
And I'm sure you walked around
wherever you wanted to go
in your red corduroy bell-bottoms.
Why not? It wasn't as if there weren't enough
red corduroy bell-bottoms to go around.
You're missing the point.
The point is we lost the Sixties and all the revolutionary
potential and the specific point is
it's your fucking fault.

It could have been anyone.
Which goes without saying.
Population is a fact of life.
Evolution is a fact.
A great number of facts.
There are more people than either of us has time for.

Fact: outer space exists.
Fact: fish are disappearing and the seas are rising.
Not quite on cue, but we all get the idea.
Giant parking lots destroy manners.
It's not really a question.
Patriarchy sucks the pleasures out of life
at an unreplenishable rate.
We agree, every drop, goes without saying,
sue me for breathing,
or let's just shut up
and wait for our fucking Coors Lite.

But can we at least agree that it didn't have to happen?
But it did.
It could have been anyone
but it was you.

Where's the remote?

SOUNDS LIKE

On top of the hill it's green,
the wifi's spotless,

there we first hear
of Jack and Jill,

and of different ways
sounds end: if Jack,

you thunk
the trunk down,

drive, up and down
the block, back and forth

across the earth
if need be,

or simply under orders,
but you can't say

Jill through to the end
without first

stopping your tongue
behind your teeth

then releasing
to let the *l* out

which lets whoever's listening
finally know

how it rhymed
with hill all along.

But if you think
sound is going to tell you

what's what,
you have another think coming.

LOVE SCENE

—to never know what you're going to say
and then to always end up saying
basically the same thing,

doesn't that get seriously old, Jack?
I love it when you call me that.

What?
Jack.

But Jack's your name, Jill said,
letting her bucket smack on top of the well water.

Pretending you don't know your name,
isn't that the same problem of compulsive improvisation

that we were just
talking about? Remember?

Touché, Jack confessed,
toujours touché.

Isn't that why we came up here?
Touché? said Jill,

I don't have a sword
and, if it comes to that,

neither do you.

BIGGER THAN BIG

Zeus savors the smoke
of perfectly spiced BBQ.

And when the really nice wine
spills on the proper surface,

that's also a thing
he greatly enjoys.

He's way up there,
but the scent arrives,

full bodied.
Like they say:

just because you're
already *on* high

no reason not to
get a little high.

Sensory bliss,
snort it.

HERA AND ZEUS AT HOME

At this point Hera thought
just how to get what she wanted.
She'd aim all his pleasure
right back at the father brother husband.
She'd knock him off his vantage.
His wishes were hateful to her.
She'd wreck his plan.

So she armored up
with oils and other irresistibles
—she'd already got hold of the love bead—
and went up the mountain
and presented herself,
like some ingénue, first time in town,
microfidgeting, hypercompliant.

As for him, never
had he felt so alive,
so on top of his game,
not when he played
badminton with Daphne,
solitaire with Lydia,
catch-the-drift with Sue,
let's make a deal with Rae,
post office with Dawn,
rolled that perfect game with Sally—
this was like the first time,
even better, it was right
before the first time
which was finally going to happen.

The cues worked to perfection.
The ground literally grew flowers
beneath them, the atmosphere
candied into a golden fog
so no one outside could really see
all that much of anything.
Sleep crept out from the branches.
Victory was hers.
Candy from a baby.

Then afterwards, when things
are a mess, his entire schedule's
shot, the beeper won't shut up,
that's precisely when
she gets to tell him, Look,
it was just sex,
I swear on our marriage bed.
Don't start.

The young know all this.
They've been hearing it since forever.
But they also know
that if you've missed the latest,
nothing you know is worth much,
that's why screens are sacred
and why it's almost physically impossible
to look away.

Miss something you're screwed.

AT THE CINEPLEX

What happens
depends on which way you face.

If you believe that Aphrodite
was one of the nicer constructions
of the human mind and nothing more,
then look right and there's Menelaus
dragging Paris by the chinstrap.
Hometeam Menelaus, the original husband,
dragging foreign loverboy Paris through the dust
to kill him and that will be that:
wife home, war's over,
property repatriated, no more epic.
Look right, and that's what's happening,
thinking Aphrodite a pleasant idea,
one of the pleasantest.

But if you can picture an embodied Aphrodite,
shaped like us but better,
divine in fact, with superpowers,
getting to change the story,
then picture this and look left
and you'll see her
swooping down and whooshing
the extremely good-looking Paris
away from the rest-area theatrics
of overaggravated types like Menelaus.

And if in the name of an active Aphrodite,
you turn all the way around,
then there's Paris already back
in the sandalwood bedroom,
pearled in a light sweat,

maybe just out dancing,
maybe just about to go,
and Aphrodite makes Helen
come to him,
and the war's back on
and the whole epic franchise.

In the bonus track, Aphrodite circles back
and drops hometeam Menelaus a note:
Drag your nemesis
as hard and slow as you like,
but after all this time don't you know
whose thumb you're under?

THE THING ABOUT RHYMES

is they always repeat
it's always up the hill

and always tumbling after
and always the same stopping place

but stopping places only last so long
and like the immortal gods

once nursery talk loses contact
with the living streams of human rememoration

once that varnish gets on you it's curtains.

THE THING ABOUT RHYMES

is that they keep happening
the same way so you can see

up turn to down
and you know you can set it up

again and follow it down again
and say Again! the second it's over

to start it back up again
because the change

is going to happen this time too.

DEATH OF AN EXTRA

There's more than just Jack and Jill rushing up the hill,
there's the camp of ripped zombies down below:

a patriarchal support group lifted to the skies
by their own prayers as they fight for zombie points

and select bevies of fleshbots.
And now some latebreaking sources are telling us

Jill never went up the hill at all
and that in fact it was Jack

who spent the whole time up there
enthralled prisoner of the web.

But whatever feed we choose,
it remains the case that, as of this writing,

there is no way of adding reliable time stamps
to anything anyone says or forwards

and until we can do that, widely and easily,
any sturdy public narrative remains a pipe dream.

But whatever Jill was doing she wasn't home,
which was fuel for endless episodes of violence

sprayed across the receiving space
with continual invention

so the audience would stay put.
Say Zombie 6 kills someone,

a well-known individual
who lived near a hotspot

and entertained spectacularly
but when Zombie 6 jumped out

spearing our one-step-slow entertainer
in the middle of the forehead,

not one of his endless guests was there
and his brains dibbled down the shaft.

SMALL

So just when you're being taken
to see the biggest big man,

just as you're being
led along with palpable dignity

by a smaller big man,
smaller by quite a bit,

smaller but still big,
suddenly some person with a badge

grabs you away
and no one ever hears anything more,

of you, that is.

DIVINE LAUGHTER

The gods' inexhaustible laughter is an Iliad formula, a minor
one, but with a modicum of hits in later centuries. It's an idea
that works in different ways, some of them nice. The gods are
laughing inexhaustibly: eternity is happy, a "their eyes, their
glittering eyes, / are gay" kind of thing, hinting at how life can
arise from matter, or providing an early glimpse of unlimited
energy, perpetual laughter betokening some inexhaustible
amusement arising from the weave of existence.

But there's also a tier-sensitive take where, OK, the gods are up
there in the skyboxes, laughing at the tragic hijinx below, while
we're down here subject to all they find so amusing. The gods like
gamers with endless free lives and us Super Marios, Ms. Pacmans,
tokens striving and dying to hold their attention.

However we hear "laughing inexhaustibly," the word "inexhaustibly"
suggests the laughter is always happening. But it only happens
twice in Homer, both times at the discomfiture of a fellow god.

First time is at the end of Book 1 of the Iliad, when Zeus
and Hera are quarreling at the banquet. Suddenly limping
tech-god Hephaistos intervenes, triggering the first outburst.

They didn't stop,
it was that funny

seeing Hephaistos
stumble out there

taking over the wine-pouring
himself, so funny him

hobbling around,
clubfeet and all,

pouring the perfect wine,
clowning and abasing

to defuse the situation
with the Big Man threatening

some really grotesque things,
the wife's eyes

wide as dinner plates.
So quick distract Big Man's

troubled mind,
grab the wine, stump around

and keep pouring,
keep them laughing,

which will kill
two birds with one stone:

1) it keeps things on the rails
and 2) it caters to the divine class,

who so enjoy being served.

THE BIRTH OF PORN

The other time the gods laugh unquenchably is in Book 8 of the
Odyssey when the bard Demodicus, the story-within-a-story
bard, a hired singer doing a brief cameo, does the one where
Aphrodite and Ares are caught in bed by the furious husband,
Hephaistos again.

He fashions a technical masterpiece,
       a completely flexible mesh
              that drops over the two flagrants,

ultrathin, ultrastrong,
       trapping them in full visibility,
              perfect focus,

no paywall,
       with the gods
              all standing around above,

laughing inexhaustibly,
       but then Hermes,
              the go-between,

thinks out loud
       how he wouldn't at all mind
              seeing himself

inside that golden picture.

IN THE KING'S BED

I love a perfect apricot,
a special thing

from the spread
of my resources,

just for you:
taste.

They used to say things
like winged words

and the fence of your teeth
right down your throat

and many other things
but words are for losers.

Taste it.

ACHILLES TO PRIAM

At the end of this whole thing
we have to get on the same page:

so listen.
Yes, I said I'm giving you

the body — but just shut up OK,
so I don't kill you,

which I know
would be exactly the wrong thing to do

and which it turns out
is just another thing

I am extremely good at:
doing the exact wrong thing

that gets everybody killed.
But, yes, the body.

Like I say,
I'm seeing to the necessities,

the washing, the oiling, the wrapping —
look, take it.

I killed him
and couldn't kill him enough,

but take it away,
go back, twelve free days.

I am promising.
Go back to your melting-pot,

all the different food,
all those languages

—good luck with that!
Like that giant water drop

hanging off your penthouse pine
and you're thinking

that it's there
and life is packed.

But surface tension
only gets you so far.

Leave. Go home.
Twelve days, no war.

Take your precious body.

BETWEEN WALLS

Down here,
when the gods do appear,

they're in control.
And if situations arise

they've got special effects
to make the winning and losing

pivot according to the Plan,
which everyone knows,

though it's hard to keep track
of all that's happening

between the various walls,
in the contested spaces outside.

But everyone already knows
how it all turns out.

The lofty walled town,
with the famous keep

and the endless scandals,
burned to the ground,

all that foreign noise,
but real parenting skills,

dense mats of local knowhow,
burned to ash,

the unpredictable entirety
of that intermeshed information

long escaped as smoke,
and us meanwhile listening

to the Plan unfolding,
the serious back and forth,

we almost lose, but of course
because it's in our language

we count ourselves among the victors,
even with the insinuating buzz of strangeness,

what we hear is ours.
But when you get to the end

and the city's not yet gone,
it's hard to be sure it was them

and not us. Because what is happening
makes it hard to credit

there ever was a plan,
hard to believe it's not going to be us

losing access to everything we know.

EPIC RULES

There're really
only two.

1) No skipping ahead.
2) No staying put.

Plus it's big,
too long to finish hearing,

while it uses
the familiar noises

to cross the blood-brain barrier
quickly, dryly,

good for long distances,
reaching across past both ends

—use your imagination,
or someone else

will be only too glad to.

LOVELINESS OF THE SELF IN TIME

Grow, grass!
Hip, hooray!
Like that!

Dry, paint!
It's really happening!
All over!

4TH TIME'S THE CHARM

can't you see the world is burning
the dream asks

haha there is no light in dreams

then doesn't the taste of the charred intelligence
of the entire species coat your tongue
offending everything it starts to say or wants to taste
the dream asks

haha you don't taste in dreams

but the mourners wailing and yelling
the dream laps at the sleeper's ear
don't these work through your mind's strongest walls

haha in dreams the ear is so warm and shut

but aren't you at least a little bit scared
a little terrified that some of these things
or newer worse things
will happen to you and everyone you know
the dream insinuates
and I couldn't agree more says the sleeper

look how tight I'm squeezing my pillow

OPTIONS

For local change, press seven.

For nature, press three.

For cultural commons, press eight.

If you've had it, press five.

For confirmation, press one.

For detraumatization, press six.

For disambiguation, press one.

To change everything but keep your body the same, press four.

To change everything, press two.

PEP TALK

Smell those apples falling?
That's your senses talking,

telling you what you already know.
Gravity rules.

But then you knew that too.
You're a lucky dog

and don't you know it!

TRUE STORY

If only we knew what we're talking about,
then actions wouldn't have to speak so much louder
than words and what a pleasant state
that is going to be!

In the meantime,
the nametag on the tree says
Homo Sapiens Sapiens and therefore

it gets sawed up and nailed back together
which happens over and over
but inside this one box, guess what?
—a stash of Fuck You Very Much t-shirts,
nearly mint.

PASSING TIME

Yawn and write

granddaughter Birdie
rubbing the bird cards on her tummy

like Athena flicking an arrow
away from a cradle

when the sky is heavy with clouds
but not too heavy since they float

CIRCULAR AUTOBIOGRAPHY

I remember my first thought.

I was a high school utopian, not horny yet I don't think,
I'd skipped a grade, was an ex-little kid not much else.
The teacher played Bach's E-major violin concerto
and for simple sounds to be exciting
was suddenly true, which was also exciting.

Flip the switch you recognize
what you never saw before.

Imagine seeing the sky,
underpants, lipstick,
things that don't mind being written down,
in fact they like it.

Like when the foot of a mountain
takes its first wobbly step,
but since that was before any writing,
we only have this mass of rumors, exciting,
though a little dull after awhile in their endless nuance.

And now look who's been sitting here the whole time:
Melancholia, frozen jangling
amid the disassembled gears and every night
she has to clean up all over again
make things artful
for tomorrow's customers streaming in
the just-up sun blasting at their backs
high as shit loving every minute

AT EMMA'S GRAVE

1

They say the mind
can keep sense alive
about seven seconds

and that we can register at most
seven things, coins, pebbles, apples,
or six, five

almost nothing.

2

Maybe that's why
we invented the present
as a place to live, to keep the things we do know,

know so exactly, keep them exactly, keep
everything, keep what we know

near, at hand, alive in our minds:
Emma.

3

It's hard to remember
what the light looked like then,

what it was saying in such detail,
hard to count the blackbirds in that pie,
the extra-special one, four and twenty they said,

but we only see the released flock, the single flying mass,
each one the first and only birth.

4

Such a small set of seconds to put everything in,
since not everything is here that we love,
which makes it impossible not to want

that small set to have been utterly different,
the flock to have swooped
right not left, to have landed

in any other tree.

5

Not the look of the light,
clear, vertical, soft, childlike,
or whatever our seven seconds say,

but how fast we've already seen
what is here, and what is not,
that's what makes the seven seconds
so hard.

6

What we see
makes us not remember
what it looked like
just a second ago
now all different
with us at a loss
with that stone there.

7

It is our privilege alone to disappear,
to never forget that we do,

never forget to set down
what must be set down

so that it not be forgotten,
not be lost in all this time:

Emma.

ONCE IS NEVER, TWICE IS ALWAYS

There's a phrase in Homeric studies: *hapax legomenon*.
Hapax = once; *legomenon* = said.

A *hapax legomenon* is a word we only see that once.
So how do we know what it means?

How do we know it's even a word?
Like in bird watching, if there's only that one-time bird,

how do you know it's a distinct species?
How do you know that one-time word

is a word at all
and not some transmission glitch?

Still, these hapaxes, these only-once words,
continued to exist,

huddled in with all the other epic noises,
lines, speeches, counterspeeches

people would hear, learn, repeat, know,
which is how we can still read

this now-stable, huge set of words.
The *Iliad* structured school days for centuries,

the massed particulars kept more or less in place
amid passing successions of heads,

each touch specific to its moment
but easy to transfer somewhere else.

So 600 years later Augustus
(just turned emperor,

in fact newly deified)
had only to quote the line

where Hector is lecturing Paris
about how truly stupid his (Paris's) sex life was

for his (Augustus's) displeasure
at daughter Julia's public gyrations

to travel down the generations to us,
for his tailored sigh

over his daughter's tedious transgressions
to go viral.

But back to hapaxes
(which are the opposite of viral).

Take Booyah!
which I first heard Stuart Scott use on TV,

praise-punctuating three pointers,
heroic accuracy: Booyah!,

like Marines expelling air
from toned, well-armed bellies

ready to defend wherever
this is now.

Booyah!
You got a problem with that?

But what about a thousand years later
when there's only

that one lonely
hapax booyah

on some tattered page?
What is it then—

boast, incantation, fuck-you, ineradicable ululation?

SOLSTICE MORNING

And so,
a little more bent,

but on the proper day,
you finally go

to the oracle
where the big reveal

turns out to be
that one and one

was really two the whole time.
And then on the way out

you get hit
with a surcharge

for being reminded
what a good investment

$2 + 2 = 4$ is.

WAKING DREAM

The day
the book of judgment

gets taken down
and read aloud

that's the day
typos will be

united with their words
while proper spellings

will be wandering
the hot streets

shouting their sins.

HOME FROM THE ORACLE

After all these years,
like Stein to my surprise

I still have to write
patriarchal poetry:

Jack and Jill
went up the hill,

which is where
they took a pill,

and which is where
they took turns, as if time

was on everyone's side.

STRAIGHT OFF THE PAGE

Off the beaten path
and off with our pants,
somewhere in a big grass acre
in a whole other country.

Not to forget it was in the past, too.

In the second place, I remember
Poe reverse-engineering "The Raven,"
"Nevermore" having the right number
and satisfying placement of affecting noises.

It really is a great word if I could stop and think.

And speaking of thinking—
if thought is tasted in the mouth,
then what is happening
when the pen tip industriously

curves and lifts
while my lips are sealed,
green open grass clearing
and us tucked somewhere in there,

sky still overhead I imagine.

APHRODITE NEVER OLD

Love of what you are
is everything

and love of what you're not
is such a stretch

that we're hard pressed
to escape the taint of the ridiculous

and we have to recognize
the power in force,

not that we have any choice.
We have to listen

when this powerful being
who loves us

so attentively
says, Watch it,

just as I lavish
so much on you now,

a little later just as easily
I might not

love you much at all,
in fact I might

loathe your sagging particulars.
Absolutely detest them, darling.

So do what I say.

WRIT IN WATER

The light was all for you today
but you only brought home
these same old posters.

Today the light was all for you
but first you lost your glasses
then you sat on them,

a bigger man than was needed
in the situation,
and though there's plenty

of blame to go around,
more than enough to warm the earth
for generations,

the light was all for you.

GOD'S OWN WORDS

still haunting the shelves
next to the bronzed baby shoes
—a tacky Youngstown tale

but after all this time
telling the body from the bathwater
stops being an obvious proposition.

And when the senses are no longer public,
then we're up shit creek, each of us
up our own privatized shit creek,

and woe to you
and woe to me
and general woe to all.

THE MUSES TO THE POETS

We just want you
to exhibit normal behavior,
think your thoughts,
reach for your favorite usables,
face your traumas
when they pulse in your neck,
scratch every itch
and in general promote
the existence of self.

Really, what we're asking
is that you make it clear
you're not some automatic attention apparatus,
prove you're not spam
or whatever word you use now,
but since proof's a game
for the half-hearted,
there's no need for you to prove anything,
just suggest it by what you sense.

Don't wait for instructions,
we like seeing you
in your natural habitat!
Any seconds you live through
are fair game.
And if one set comes back
like some prodigal offspring,
begging for another chance,
entertain the whole proposition generously,
remember everything, it's all good.

Even your data amuses us,
as does the smell
of burning fat from your sacrifices,
successful or otherwise,
as do your wars,
as do your pretty orgasms,
but if you really want to know,
none of it holds our attention forever.

ACKNOWLEDGEMENT

Some of these words
have appeared in the following places:

my mind, tongue, ear and files,
and in the minds, tongues, ears and files

of loved ones, friends, acquaintances,
the wide world I've heard

and not heard,
flyers on the sidewalk,

billboards lit and peeling,
oceanic screens and private polling places,

any other mouth the ideal location
to hear these words

transing, flaunting, sniffing, standing at attention,
beaten into twitchy sameness,

moodily bowing to the monotonies
of the convinced lash.

The bodies of these words
stretched out seemingly endless but animated

like the green hills lining the freeways
in New Jersey or Indiana,

half-mile hills thirty feet high
you glide by

and out the windshield,
suddenly there's the dull stub

of a small smokestack,
a little grey tube stuck

in the middle of this next elongated green lump,
and then not long after,

another one slides behind,
each tube expressing

its own signature output
of the slowly cooking plastic

and fatigued newsprint
secreted beneath the undulating

green hills offgassing
the invisible news,

our sacred intoxicant.

FROM THE GENERAL FUND

Charge up,
  be reborn,
    do this to yourself.

Wind down,
  stop faking,
    quit while you're at
    least somewhere.

Push on,
  act your age,
    hope no one notices.

Cut down,
  breathe deep,
    no amount of clicking
    will do what you want.

Expect the same,
  change your mind,
    think.

Think twice,
  then see what happens,
    in general if not to you.

NATURE DOMINATRIX

Nabokov the chronophobe is dead
and we are each alive.

Cobwebs stretching over chamomile buds
white with dew nothing to do

with you or me.
I remember how Nabokov described his first poem.

It was in prose,
god knows what went on

behind the curtain,
but the words said something about

a sunny sky right after a storm
and a glance out the window showed a drop

of three-minute-old rainwater
spilling down the spine of a leaf,

dripping off so the leaf sprang back,
but it only happens that once

and has no name.

THE MAITRE D'S TALE

This one mother comes in,
going on about her little boy,

no future, he'll be handing
the winners their drinks,

and when he meets the old remnants,
there'll be at best a sideways kiss,

maybe he gets his lips wet,
but nothing to swallow,

which you hear out attentively,
then after the proper interval,

you bring the menu
like for everybody else.

The schedule
doesn't shut down

just because the sky falls.
And since this is your one night,

you should remember Troy
in the best sense,

the swagger of the swoops,
the dependability of the connectors,

the sidelit mist hovering above the Hudson
through the remaining peepholes,

you get a quick glimpse
of time spread out

like a fresh stiff tablecloth—
it is a conscious universe after all,

and you do have reservations.

HEY DAVID

but you can't hear.
All that witty impatience
shut under earth's lid,
adding to the changing mass.

Sharable libraries at the tips of our tongues,
back when you had one,
earth's lid—
you'd instantly

hear the joke about lids,
ten-dollar bags,
old easy-going dope,
pot, did we say?

We wouldn't have
called each other by name,
why invoke the name
when there's time?

THE PLOT THICKENS

1

Jack and Jill may well
have gone up the hill

but there are many hills,
many with their tops removed

for all to see,
leaving nothing to the imagination.

Hills are the closest things you see
from the air.

2

Don't act surprised,
but Torture and Terror

were just here,
chained together, pretending

they didn't know each other.
They were never shy gods,

but here it was like
they were trying to blend in

with the debris, taking advantage
of the spectacle

of the couple
climbing the hill

3

Since generosity
always makes for the cleanest way out

then of course let us wish
Jack and Jill the fullest

employment of their subjectivities
—but aren't happy endings

just asking for it?

ABC'S

There was no need for an Iliad
and there was not enough time

to hear the whole thing,
but once it existed

or began existing,
once the big set of moments,

interlocked scenes, arguments, continuity paste,
words hammered into shiny rhythmic clumps,

short sobering lessons,
reproducible tableaux,

the cast of all powerful gods
but of course totally human,

except all powerful, which goes
without saying, once

all this began happening and then,
though the record skips,

nevertheless the precision is audible
and needs to be kept going

from mouth to ear to mind to hand
and tracking back with revisions and elisions

and everyone's faulty memories,
weak links everywhere,

the library burns,
the equipment

obsolescent
the minute you take it out of the box,

plus people are stressed
by the ridiculous overbooking,

but, still, it—the whole poem—
gets said and resaid

eventually into longterm memory,
which is why, so long after

we've each been weaned
into our one-of-a-kind

need-to-know outposts,
why we still speak in formulas.

Be that as it may,
eventually one fine day

we finally get to the end of Book 4
where the serious killing begins:

A kills B
and then as A's friend C

goes to seize B's armor,
D kills C.

General fighting
over C's body.

And here now is mighty E
killing F,

crushing him in gruesome detail,
and this death

prompts G to throw his spear
straight at E,

but instead of E, it's H
who's instantly

shorn of light,
its insistent pleasures chopped off,

the dependable uploads
gone just like that,

the huge downloads so automatic,
all that change

with the one slash
stopped for H,

who still had so much
to think about,

and this enrages
mighty I,

the legitimately famous I,
who then, bulging

with mania, kills J,
J of all people,

that fun-loving nobody,
born like us

in the midst of the alphabet.

POSTLUDE

Afterwards, Memory sighed in Desire's ear,
sweetheart, you still awake?

So, OK, don't you finally have to admit
that the present gets just plain *boring*?

Tell me about it sweetheart!
broke in Desire, I *know*, all the *novelty*,
the inertia, everything such a struggle,
the beads of sweat, focus so tight
you can't see anything else,
what kind of somnambulists do they take us for?
—Sweetheart, now *you're* asleep!

Insomniacs? suggested Memory.

I always mean exactly what I say, said Desire,
why else take the trouble?
No, what I'm saying is these presentists
with their foreboding music,
then the warriors come striding out,
these entrepreneurs must think everybody's
always in imminent danger of narcolepsy
and that you can only see
when you're being hit over the head
tight focus, traumatic closeups,
organs cut out, sharp angles,
—sword slashes, they *love* sword slashes,
blades in general, the glints
swirling down the surface,
and they have to stay inventive,
the eyeball on a speartip,
the multiple eyeballs rolling in the dust,

the schools of fish flashing up
nibbling the kidney that used to be
inside our latest protagonist,
anything to keep us glued
because it's the present.

Well,—Memory waiting
to make sure nothing more was coming,
well, come *on,*
you know you're the worst insomniac,
thrashing around like you do.
You keep us both up.

Let's see if anything else is on, sighed Desire,
—if either of us can work these fucking remotes, that is.

No, Memory counseled, let's let sleeping dogs lie.
Technologies are only out for themselves.

GLASS HALF-FULL

They say Jack and Jill
went up the hill

to fetch a pail of water
without a thought in the world

of who might be up there already,
involved as they were

with each other's detail,
"to *fetch* a *pail* of *wa* ter" —

that's the empty bucket swinging,
which they're probably

taking turns carrying,
passing it back and forth,

shy at the moment of transfer.
When arousal begins

some faculties sharpen
while others are dampened,

to repeat what everyone knows,
but none of our senses

will be reliable guides
for what they say

happened next:
Jack fell down

and broke his crown
and Jill came tumbling after.

Hardly what you'd call
a triumphal second act.

Breaking your crown never helps,
rivulets of trauma

blotching down the hill
and nothing's going to work

the same anymore.
But what about Jill tumbling after?

No mention in her case
of any head trauma,

and doesn't tumbling suggest
she's something of an acrobat

with the ability to accommodate
to upside-down situations

and doesn't that hold out hope
that we can develop portable scales

for weighing unlike things?

TACT IN TROY

In the early twenty-first century
we're still finding out about our miraculous powers
amid this jumbled crowd of hulking buildings,
ton upon ton of exquisitely priced brick,
chrome spun almost too fine to see,
the entire weight of this exacting knowledge
so easy for our miracle bombs to blow up,
which everybody knows but has presents to get
and other friendly things to do
because we like each other as much as ever.

Notes

12 "Armor Swap"
The latter part of the poem follows the contours of an episode in
Book 6 of the *Iliad*, lines 119-236 (i.e., 6.119-36), though consider-
ably sped up. The Greek Diomedes encounters Glaucon (enemy,
Trojan ally) in battle and challenges him with great sarcasm.
However, in the midst of their ritual declarations of hostility they
discover they're distant relatives and thus in some ineradicable sense
on the same side. The episode ends with Glaucon trading his gold
armor for Diomedes' bronze: like trading 100 oxen for 9, we're told.
  "Contrary to romantic clichés, the Homeric warrior is not the
opposite of the haggling shopkeeper. Exchange, negotiation of
disputes, and settlements are honourable transactions in the
Homeric world, to be carried both with a keen calculation of
material advantage and with a deep sense of ceremony. The action
of the Iliad, however, shows the collapse of procedures for resolving
conflicts." Martin Mueller, *The Iliad*.
  Iliad scholar G.S. Kirk says the entire episode is a deliberate
swerve out of epic narrative into the extravagance of folk-tale.

18 "Aphrodite and Helen"
This is loosely based on the dialog between the two in 3.399-418.

20 "Mister Big"
This is as close as anything in the book comes to translation, though
it's still extremely loose. I'm trying to produce the effect of one of the
weirdest Homeric similes: the lines in 4.141-147. Menelaus is ambushed
by an enemy archer; Athena saves him by a deflection of the arrow
described in extended detail. His thigh is grazed; the blood that
escapes is compared to an expensive purple horse-ornament.

22 "Paganism for Dummies"
The last lines of the poem refer to the end of the Iliad, (Book 24),
where the Trojan king Priam comes to the Greek Achilles to beg for
the body of his son Hector.
  Zeus weeps for his mortal son Sarpedon at 16.459. Bloody tears
falling from the sky are an early special effect.

25 "All-Purpose Disaster Poem"
This originated when a colleague at Penn, Emily Steiner, asked
some of us on the faculty along with her undergraduate class to
write in response to a chunk of *Beowolf*, a tale within a tale where
there's a murder at a wedding party, but the next morning both
clans are iced in and stuck with each in the same space for the whole
long winter. At least that's what I think the excerpt was saying: I
never actually made it through the assigned lines — sorry, Emily —
before I was struck by the scenario of antagonists suspended in
nonantagonism.

   At more or less the same time, I'd just read Charles Bernstein's
Recalculating, and the line "It's your fucking fault" (from "Morality")
seemed irresistibly apropos.

32 "Hera and Zeus at Home"
This is a retelling of "The Beguilement of Zeus" in Book 14, where
Hera seduces her husband in order to divert his attention from the
battlefield, where he's been helping the Trojans, whom Hera
loathes.

34 "At The Cineplex"
This is based on the odd narrative twist near the beginning of Book
3, where just as we expect the opening of the initial battle between
the massed armies of Greeks and Trojans, suddenly Paris jumps out
and proposes a duel with the winner taking Helen and the armies
going home. Menalaus eagerly accepts this turn of events, which
would create an impossible result and would shortcircuit the Iliad as
an epic (which has to be big and at this point has 20 books to go). This
kind of narrative feint on the poet's part is called the "epic almost."

   The duel begins and quickly Paris is about to killed when, in
very few lines, Aphrodite swoops down, gathers him up and deposits
him in his bedroom in Troy. Then Aphrodite more or less shoves
Helen to join Paris.

38 "Death of an Extra"
Jill not actually being at Troy is a swerving mention of the meme
of Helen not actually being at Troy and therefore of the blood-
drenched ten-year siege being in service of a phantom image. The

fifth-century BCE poet Stesichorus first wrote a poem blaming Helen for the war and was punished with blindness, then wrote a palinode (recantation) where the actual Helen was in Egypt and her phantom was at Troy. He regained his sight. Later, there's Euripides's *Helen in Egypt*; much later, H.D.'s *Helen in Egypt* and Anne Carson's *Autobiography of Red*.

40 "Small"
There are many small (temporary) personages in the *Iliad*. Here are two, from Richard Janko's commentary re 14.442-53 (a killing scene): "His father, 'Brilliant', is a nobody dignified by the repetition of his name"; and "His father, Areilukos, looks like an *ad hoc* invention to fit the meter."

45 "Achilles to Priam"
This is based on the Achilles-Priam meeting in Book 24.

57 "At Emma's Grave"
This was written for the yarzheit ceremony for Emma Bee Bernstein.

60 "Once Is Never, Twice is Always"
The title comes from a remark I read somewhere by the *Iliad* scholar and philologist Wilamovitz.
    The line Augustus quoted (3.40) is, roughly, "Better you never existed, better you'd died unwed."

67 "Aphrodite Never Old"
This is loosely based on the same passage as "Aphrodite and Helen," but zeroes in on the end (3.413-420).

77 "Maitre D's Tale"
The beginning echoes Andromache's lament, especially 22.490-496.